APPLICATION OF

PETER CHEW THEOREM

TO GEOMETRY (DISTANCE)

PETER CHEW

PCET VENTURES (003368687-P)

Email:peterchew999@hotmail.my

© Peter Chew 2023

Cover Design : Peter Chew

Cover Image: Freepik Premium

Mathematician, Inventor and Biochemist Peter Chew

Peter Chew is Mathematician, Inventor and Biochemist. Global issue analyst, Reviewer for Europe Publisher, Engineering Mathematics Lecturer and President of Research and Development Secondary School (IND) for Kedah State Association [2015-18].

Peter Chew received the Certificate of appreciation from Malaysian Health Minister Datuk Seri Dr. Adam Baba(2021), PSB Singapore. National QC Convention STAR AWARD (2 STAR), 2019 Outstanding Analyst Award from IMRF (International Multidisciplinary Research Foundation), IMFR Inventor Award 2020 , the Best Presentation Award at the 8th

International Conference on Engineering Mathematics and Physics ICEMP 2019 in Ningbo, China , Excellent award (Silver) of the virtual International, Invention, Innovation & Design Competition 2020 (3iDC2020) and Jury in the International Teaching and Learning Invention, Innovation Competition (iTaLiiC2023).

Analytical articles published in local and international media. Author for more than 60 Books , 8 preprint articles published in the World Health Organization (WHO) and 36 article published in the Europe PMC.

Peter Chew also is CEO PCET, Ventures, Malaysia, PCET is a long research associate of IMRF (International Multidisciplinary Research Foundation), Institute of higher Education & Research with its HQ at India and Academic Chapters all over the world, PCET also Conference Partner in CoSMEd2021 by SEAMEO RECSAM.

Peter Chew as 2nd Plenary Speaker the 6th International Multidisciplinary Research Conference with a Mindanao Zonal Assembly on January 14, 2023, at the Immaculate Conception University, Bajada Campus, Davao City.

Keynote Speaker of the 8th International Conference on Computer Engineering and Mathematical Sciences (ICCEMS 2019) , the International Conference on Applications of Physics , Chemistry & Engineering Sciences, ICPCE 2020 , 2nd Global Summit on Public Health and Preventive Medicine (GSPHPM2023) June 19, 2023 and World BIOPOLYMERS & POLYMER CHEMISTRY CONGRESS" 10-11 July 2023 | Online by Drug Delivery,

Special Talk Speaker at the 2019 International Conference on Advances in Mathematics, Statistics and Computer Science, the 100th CONF of the IMRF,2019, Goa , India.

Invite Speaker of the 24th Asian Mathematical Technology Conference (ATCM 2019) Leshan China , the 5^{th}(2020), 6th (2021) and 7th (2022) International Conference on Management, Engineering, Science, Social Sciences and Humanities by Society For Research Development(SRD) and 12th International Conference on Engineering Mathematics and Physics (July 5-7, 2023 in Kuala Lumpur, Malaysia).

Peter Chew is also Program Chair for the 11th International Conference on Engineering Mathematics and Physics (ICEMP 2022, Saint-Étienne, France | July 7-9, 2022) and Program Chair for the 12th International Conference on Engineering Mathematics and Physics (ICEMP 2023, Kuala Lumpur, Malaysia | July 5-7, 2023).

For more information, please get it from this link Orcid: https://orcid.org/0000-0002-5935-3041.

APPLICATION OF PETER CHEW THEOREM FOR GEOMETRY(DISTANCE)

8

APPLICATION OF PETER CHEW THEOREM FOR GEOMETRY(DISTANCE)

TABLE OF CONTENTS

3. Geometry(Distance) ... 31
  3.1 Distance between two points ... 31
  3.2 Distance between Point and Lines ... 34
  3.3 Distance between Two Parallel Lines ... 36
4. Application of Peter Chew Theorem for Geometry (Distance) ... 38
  4.1 Distance between two points ... 38
  4.2 Distance between Point and Line ... 50
  4.3 Distance between Two Parallel Lines ... 58
5. Conclusion ... 66
6. Reference ... 67

Application of Peter Chew Theorem

for Geometry(Distance)

Abstract. :

Presenting numbers in Surd form is quite common in science and engineering especially where a calculator is either not allowed or unavailable, and the calculations to be undertaken involve irrational values.

The purpose of Peter Chew Theorem For Quadratic Surds is to let upcoming generation solve same problem of Quadratic Surd can solve simple and directly compare what`s now solution.

Therefore, the application of Peter Chew Theorem in Geometry (Distance) can make the teaching and learning of Geometry easier.

The purpose of Peter Chew Theorem is the same as Albert Einstein's famous quote **Everything should be made as simple as possible , but not simpler.**

Chapter 1: Peter Chew Theorem[1]

1.1 Current Methods and Peter Chew Theorem Conversion Quadratic Surd

Current Method , there are two methods conversion Quadratic Surd on text book ;

i) Quadratic surds method,

For $\sqrt{a \pm 2\sqrt{b}}$, $x + y = a$, $xy = b$ $(a, b, x, y > 0)$.

$$\sqrt{a \pm 2\sqrt{b}} = \sqrt{x + y \pm 2\sqrt{xy}}$$

$$= \sqrt{(\sqrt{x})^2 + (\sqrt{y})^2 \pm 2\sqrt{xy}}$$

$$= \sqrt{(\sqrt{x} \pm \sqrt{y})^2}$$

$$= \sqrt{x} \pm \sqrt{y} , \quad (x > y > 0).$$

If we can know two positive integers x and y such that the sum of x and y equals a and the product of x and y equals b, then we usually use the Quadratic Surds method. Therefore, $\sqrt{(a \pm 2\sqrt{b})} = \sqrt{x} \pm \sqrt{y}$, $x > y > 0$.

However, if the values of a and b are large, the Quadratic Surds method is not suitable because it is difficult to know which two positive integers x and y make the sum of x and y equal to a and the product of x and y equal to b . Therefore, for large values of a and b, textbooks often recommend comparison methods.

ii) the Comparison method.

Let $\sqrt{a \pm 2\sqrt{b}} = \sqrt{x} \pm \sqrt{y}$, $x > y > 0$

Squaring gives, $a \pm 2\sqrt{b} = x + y \pm 2\sqrt{xy}$

By Comparison, $a = x + y$ ...i), $b = x\, y$...ii)

Solve i) and ii), get the value x and y.

iii)   Peter Chew Theorem

Peter Chew Theorem is knowledge in the age of AI that makes it easier and faster to convert any value of Quadratic Surds.

If roots of $x^2 - ax + b = 0$ are α *and* β, then $\sqrt{a \pm 2\sqrt{b}} = \sqrt{\alpha} \pm \sqrt{\beta}$, where $\alpha > \beta$

Note : Peter Chew Theorem is also a simple knowledge.

1.2 Convert the Quadratic Surds into the sum or difference of two real numbers

a) For small value Quadratic Surds.

Example: Find $\sqrt{11 + 2\sqrt{28}}$ in the form $\sqrt{x} + \sqrt{y}$,

where $x > y > 0$

Current Method,

i) Solution 1:

$$\sqrt{11 + 2\sqrt{28}} = \sqrt{7 + 4 + 2\sqrt{(7)(4)}}$$

$$= \sqrt{(\sqrt{7})^2 + (\sqrt{4})^2 + 2\sqrt{(7)(4)}}$$

$$= \sqrt{(\sqrt{7} + \sqrt{4})^2}$$

$$= \sqrt{7} + 2$$

ii) Solution 2: Let $\sqrt{11 + 2\sqrt{28}}$ be $\sqrt{x} + \sqrt{y}$

$$11 + 2\sqrt{28} = (\sqrt{x} + \sqrt{y})^2$$

$$= x + y + 2\sqrt{xy}$$

Comparing the two sides of the above equation,

we have $x + y = 11$

$$y = 11 - x \ \dots \text{ i)}$$

And $\qquad xy = 28 \quad \dots\dots\text{ii)}$

Substitute i) in ii), $\quad x(11 - x) = 28$

$$11x - x^2 = 28$$

$$x^2 - 11x + 28 = 0$$

$$(x - 4)(x - 7) = 0$$

$$x = 4, 7$$

From i), When $x = 4$, $y = 11 - 4 = 7$

When $x = 7$, $y = 11 - 7 = 4$

$$\therefore \ \sqrt{11 + 2\sqrt{28}} = \sqrt{7} + \sqrt{4}$$

$$= \sqrt{7} + 2$$

iii)   Peter Chew Theorem,

Cause $x^2 - 11x + 28 = 0$, then $x = 4, 7$

$$\therefore \ \sqrt{11 + 2\sqrt{28}} = \sqrt{7} + \sqrt{4}$$

$$= \sqrt{7} + 2$$

b) For large value Quadratic Surds.

Example:

Find $\sqrt{80235 + 2\sqrt{838102050}}$ in the form $\sqrt{x} + \sqrt{y}$,

where $x > y > 0$

Current Method

i) Solution 1: Not suitable

ii) Solution 2:

Let $\sqrt{1832 + 2\sqrt{679855}}$ be $\sqrt{x} + \sqrt{y}$

$$1832 + 2\sqrt{679855} = (\sqrt{x} + \sqrt{y})^2$$

$$= x + y + 2\sqrt{xy}$$

Comparing the two sides of the above equation,

We have $\quad x + y = 1832$

$$y = 1832 - x \ldots.. i)$$

And $\quad x\,y = 679855 \quad \ldots......ii)$

Substitute *i) in ii)*, $\quad x(1832 - x) = 679855$

$$1832x - x^2 = 679855$$

$$x^2 - 1832x + 679855 = 0$$

$$(x - 1315)(x - 517) = 0$$

$$x = 1315, 517$$

From *i)*, When x = 1315, y = 1832 − 1315 = 517

When x = 517, y = 1832 − 517 = 1315

$$\therefore \ \sqrt{1832 + 2\sqrt{679855}} \ = \sqrt{1315} + \sqrt{517}$$

iii)   Peter Chew Theorem

Cause $x^2 - 1832x + 679855 = 0,$

$$\text{then } x = 1315, 517$$

$$\therefore \ \sqrt{1832 + 2\sqrt{679855}} \ = \sqrt{1315} + \sqrt{517}$$

1.3 Convert the square root of a complex number into a complex number.

Convert the square root of a complex number into a complex number (the sum or difference between the real part and the imaginary part).

Because the square root of the complex number is also the quadratic surd ($\sqrt{a + bi} = \sqrt{a + b\sqrt{-1}}$).

Current Method,

Example:

Find $\sqrt{-3 + 4i}$ in the form $\sqrt{x} + \sqrt{y}\,i$, where $x, y > 0$.

i)   Solution 1 : Not suitable

ii)   Solution 2:

let $\sqrt{-3 + 4i} = (\sqrt{x} + \sqrt{y}\,i)$.   (x, y > 0)

$-3 + 4i = x - y + 2\sqrt{xy}\,i$

Comparing the two sides of the above equation,

We have $\qquad$ x - y = -3

$$y = x+3 \ ..... \ i)$$

And $\qquad$ $2 \sqrt{xy} = 4$

$$xy = 4 \quad ....ii)$$

Substitute i) in ii), $\quad$ x (x+3) = 4

$$x^2 + 3x = 4$$

$$x^2 + 3x - 4 = 0$$

$$x = 1, -4 \ (\text{reject} \ x, y>0)$$

From i), When x = 1, y = 1 + 3 = 4

$$\therefore \quad z = (\sqrt{1} + \sqrt{4} \ i)$$

$$= (1 + 2 \ i)$$

iii) $\quad$ **Peter Chew Theorem,** $\sqrt{-3 + 4i} = \sqrt{-3 + 2\sqrt{-4}}$

Cause $\quad x^2 + 3x - 4 = 0$, then x = 1, − 4

$$\therefore \ \sqrt{-3 + 4i} = (\sqrt{1} + \sqrt{-4})$$

$$= (1 + 2 \ i)$$

1.4 Convert the Quadratic Surds into the sum or difference of two complex numbers.

Example 1: Find $\sqrt{2 + 2\sqrt{5}}$ in the form $\sqrt{z} + \sqrt{\bar{z}}$,

i) **Solution 1:** Not suitable

ii) **Solution 2:** Let $\sqrt{2 + 2\sqrt{5}}$ be $\sqrt{x} + \sqrt{y}$

$$2 + 2\sqrt{5} = (\sqrt{x} + \sqrt{y})^2$$
$$= x + y + 2\sqrt{xy}$$

Comparing the two sides of the above equation,

we have $\quad x + y = 2$

$$y = 2 - x \; ..... \; i)$$

And $\quad\quad xy = 5 \quad ....ii)$

Substitute i) in ii), $x(2 - x) = 5$

$$2x - x^2 = 5$$

$$x^2 - 2x + 5 = 0$$

$$x = 1+2i, \ 1-2i$$

From i),

When $x = 1+2i$, $y = 2 - (1+2i) = 1 - 2i$

When $x = 1-2i$, $y = 2 - (1-2i) = 1 + 2i$

$$\therefore \ \sqrt{2 + 2\sqrt{15}} \ = \ \sqrt{1 + 2i} + \sqrt{1 - 2i}$$

iii)   **Peter Chew Theorem,**

`Cause $x^2 - 2x + 5 = 0$, then $x = 1+2i, \ 1-2i$

$$\therefore \ \sqrt{2 + 2\sqrt{5}} \ = \ \sqrt{1 + 2i} + \sqrt{1 - 2i}$$

Example 2: Find $\sqrt{4 + 2\sqrt{9}}$ **in the form** $\sqrt{z} + \sqrt{\bar{z}}$,

---

i)   **Solution 1:** Not suitable

ii)   **Solution 2:** Let $\sqrt{4 + 2\sqrt{9}}$ be $\sqrt{x} + \sqrt{y}$

$$4 + 2\sqrt{9} = (\sqrt{x} + \sqrt{y})^2$$

$$= x + y + 2\sqrt{xy}$$

Comparing the two sides of the above equation,

we have $x + y = 4$

$$y = 4 - x \text{ ..... i)}$$

And $xy = 9 \text{ ....ii)}$

Substitute i) in ii), $x (4 - x) = 9$

$$4x - x^2 = 9$$

$$x^2 - 4x + 9 = 0$$

$$x = 2+3i, \ 2-3i$$

From i),

When x =2+3i, y = 4 - (2+3i) =2 - 3i

When x =2-3i, y = 4 - (2-3i) =2 + 3i

$$\therefore \ \sqrt{4 + 2\sqrt{9}} \ = \ \sqrt{2 + 3i} + \sqrt{2 - 3i}$$

iii)   **Peter Chew Theorem,**

`Cause $x^2 - 4x + 9 = 0$, then x = 2+3i, 2-3i

$$\therefore \ \sqrt{4 + 2\sqrt{9}} \ = \ \sqrt{2 + 3i} + \sqrt{2 - 3i}$$

Chapter 2: **Application of Peter Chew Theorem for Geometry (Distance)**

1. INTRODUCTION

1.1 Presenting numbers in surd form is quite common in Science and Engineering. [1]

Presenting numbers in *surd* form is quite common in science and engineering especially where a calculator is either not allowed or unavailable, and the calculations to be undertaken involve irrational values.

We will be looking at this form of representation of numbers and how to carry out their calculations. One thing I should add at this point, and which you will soon come to know better, is that surds share many things in common with complex numbers. Consequently, understanding one of the two will facilitate learning the other.

1.2 Surds Explained with Worked Examples(pg 30)

In a triangle ABC, $\quad$ AB $=$ BC $= \left(\sqrt{3} - 1\right)cm$ $\quad$ and $\angle ACB =$ 30^0 , without using a calculator find the length of AC. Figure 5.

Solution

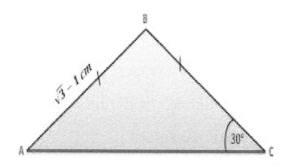

Figure 5

Where AB $= c = \left(\sqrt{3} - 1\right)cm,$

$\quad$ BC $= a = \left(\sqrt{3} - 1\right)cm$

$\quad$ AC $= b$

Also, $\angle BAC = \angle ACB = 30^0$.

$$AB = BC$$

$$\angle B = 180^0 - (\angle BAC + \angle BAC)$$

$$= 120^0$$

We can now find AC as

$b^2 \quad = \quad (\sqrt{3} - 1)^2 + (\sqrt{3} - 1)^2 - 2(\sqrt{3} - 1)(\sqrt{3} - 1)\cos 120^0$.

$$= 2(\sqrt{3} - 1)^2 - 2(\sqrt{3} - 1)^2(-\cos 60^0)$$

$$= 2[3 + 1 - 2\sqrt{3}] - 2[3 + 1 - 2\sqrt{3}](-\tfrac{1}{2})$$

$$= 2[4 - 2\sqrt{3}] + [4 - 2\sqrt{3}]$$

$$= 3[4 - 2\sqrt{3}]$$

$$= 12 - 6\sqrt{3}$$

$$b = \sqrt{12 - 6\sqrt{3}}$$

Let the square root of the $12 - 6\sqrt{3}$ be $\sqrt{x} - \sqrt{y}$ for which x, y $\in$R. Therefore

$$12 - 6\sqrt{3} = (\sqrt{x} - \sqrt{y})^2$$

$$= x + y - 2\sqrt{xy}$$

Comparing the two sides of the above equation,

We have $x + y = 12$

And $\quad -2\sqrt{xy} = -6\sqrt{3}$

Divide both sides by -2, $\quad \sqrt{xy} = 3\sqrt{3}$

Square both sides, $\quad xy = 27$ ....(ii)

From (i), $y = 12 - x$ ....(iii)

Substitute equation (iii) in equation (ii),

$$x(12 - x) = 27$$

$$12x - x^2 = 27.$$

$$x^2 - 12x + 27 = 0$$

$$(x - 9)(x - 3) = 0$$

Therefore, either $x - 9 = 0$, $x - 3 = 0$

$$x = 9, 3$$

We now need to find the corresponding values for y, thus

When x = 9, from (iii), y = 12 -9 = 3 .

And when x = 3 , from (iii) , y = 12 − 3 = 9

Hence , the square root of the $12 - 6\sqrt{3}$ are

$$\sqrt{x} - \sqrt{y} = \sqrt{9} - \sqrt{3}$$

$$= 3 - \sqrt{3}$$

and $\sqrt{a} + \sqrt{b} = \sqrt{3} - \sqrt{9}$

$$= \sqrt{3} - 3$$

$$\therefore \sqrt{12 - 6\sqrt{3}} = \pm (3 - \sqrt{3}).$$

Since the length AC can only be a positive value,

then only answer here is AC = (3 − $\sqrt{3}$) cm .   [$\sqrt{3}$ −

3 is negative].

2 Peter Chew Theorem^2 for Quadratic Surds

The Objectives Peter Chew Theorem^2 is to let upcoming generation solve same problem of quadratic roots can solve directly and more easy compare what's now solution.

Therefore, the application of Peter Chew's theorem in **Electrical Engineering** can make the teaching and learning of **Electrical Engineering** easier.

2.1 Prove of Peter Chew Theorem [3,4]

If roots of $x^2 - ax + b = 0$ are α and β,

Veda's theorem,

$$\alpha + \beta = -\frac{-a}{1} = a \ \text{.....i)}, \qquad \alpha\beta = \frac{b}{1} = b \ \text{........ii)}.$$

$$(\sqrt{\alpha} \pm \sqrt{\beta})^2 = \alpha + \beta \pm 2\sqrt{\alpha}\sqrt{\beta}$$

$$= a \pm 2\sqrt{b}$$

$$(\sqrt{\alpha} \pm \sqrt{\beta}) = \sqrt{a \pm 2\sqrt{b}} \ , \ \alpha > \beta > 0$$

$$\therefore \ \sqrt{a \pm 2\sqrt{b}} = \sqrt{\alpha} \pm \sqrt{\beta} \ \text{where} \ \alpha > \beta > 0.$$

2.2 Current Method and Peter Chew Theorem

Current Method . At present, there are two methods for solving the problem of the Quadratic Surds; they are the Quadratic Surds method and the Comparison method.

If we can find two positive integers x and y such that the sum of x and y is equal to a, and the product of x and y is equal to b, then we usually use Quadratic Surds method. Therefore,

$$\sqrt{a \pm 2\sqrt{b}} = \sqrt{x} \pm \sqrt{y} \quad , x > y > 0.$$

However, if the values   of a and b are large, it is not suitable to use Quadratic Surds method.

i) Quadratic surds method, .for $\sqrt{a \pm 2\sqrt{b}}$, $x + y = a$, $xy = b$ $(a, b, x, y > 0)$.

$$\sqrt{a \pm 2\sqrt{b}} = \sqrt{x + y \pm 2\sqrt{xy}}$$

$$= \sqrt{(\sqrt{x})^2 + (\sqrt{y})^2 \pm 2\sqrt{xy}}$$

$$= \sqrt{(\sqrt{x} \pm \sqrt{y})^2}$$

$$= \sqrt{x} \pm \sqrt{y}, \quad (x > y > 0).$$

For large value and complex root, this method not suitable.

ii) Comparison method, Let $\sqrt{a \pm 2\sqrt{b}} = \sqrt{x} \pm \sqrt{y}$, $x > y > 0$

Squaring gives, $a \pm 2\sqrt{b} = x + y \pm 2\sqrt{xy}$

By Comparison, $a = x + y$ ...i), $b = x\,y$...ii). Solve i) and ii), get x and y.

iii)   Peter Chew Theorem : If roots of $x^2 - ax + b = 0$

are α **and** β, then $\sqrt{a \pm 2\sqrt{b}} = \sqrt{\alpha} \pm \sqrt{\beta}$,where $\alpha > \beta$

3 Geometry(Distance)

3.1 Distance between two points

Distance between two points formula.[5]

Distance between two points formula uses the coordinates of two points in space. In coordinate geometry, the distance between two points can be calculated using distance formula, present in a two-dimensional or three-dimensional space. The distance formula for two points is also an application of the Pythagoras theorem. Let us learn more in this article with examples.

What is Distance Between Two Points Formula?

Distance between two points is the length of the line segment that connects the two points in a plane. The formula to find the distance between the two points is usually given by $d = \sqrt{(x_2 - x_1)^2 + (y_2 - y_1)^2}$. This formula is used to find the distance between any two points on a coordinate plane or x-y plane.

$$D = \sqrt{(x_2 - x_1)^2 + (y_2 - y_1)^2}$$

Q.1: What is the distance between two points A and B whose coordinates are (3, 2) and (9, 7), respectively?

Solution: Given, A (3,2) and B(9,7) are the two points in a plane. We have to find the distance between A and B.Using distance between formula for two points, we know;

Distance, $d = \sqrt{(x_2 - x_1)^2 + (y_2 - y_1)^2}$.

Here, $x_1 = 3$, $x_2 = 9$, $y_1 = 2$ and $y_2 = 7$.

Thus, putting all the values of x and y in the formula, we get;

$d = \sqrt{(9-3)^2 + (7-2)^2}$

$d = \sqrt{36 + 25}$

$d = \sqrt{61}$ unit.

Solved Examples.

Example : Find the distance of the point (4, –6) from the line 2x – 7y – 24 = 0.

Solution:

Given line is $2x - 7y - 24 = 0$. ...... (1)

Comparing (1) with general equation of line Ax + By + C = 0, we get

A = 2, B = –7 and C = –24.

Given point is $(x_1, y_1) = (4, -6)$.

The distance of the given point from given line is

$$d = \frac{\left|2(4) - 7(-6) - 24\right|}{\sqrt{2^2 + (-7)^2}}.$$

$$= \frac{26}{7.28}.$$

$$= 3.6$$

3.3 Distance between Two Parallel Lines.[7]

The two parallel lines can be taken in the form

$y = mx + c_1$ .... (i)

and $y = mx + c_2$ .... (ii)

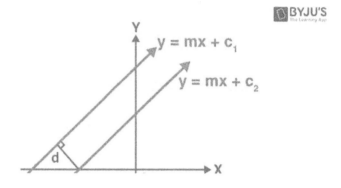

Distance d between two parallel lines $y = mx + c_1$ and $y = mx + c_2$ is given by

$$d = \frac{|c_2 - c_1|}{\sqrt{a^2 + b^2}}.$$

Considering the following equations of 2 parallel lines, we can calculate the distance between those lines using the distance formula

$ax + by + c = 0$

$ax + by + C_1 = 0$

Using the above 2 equations, we can conclude that

Distance between 2 parallel lines, $d = \dfrac{|c - c_1|}{\sqrt{a^2 + b^2}}$

Example: Calculate the distance between the parallel lines $3x + 4y + 7 = 0$ & $3x + 4y - 5 = 0$.

Solution:

The distance between two parallel lines is given by d

$= \dfrac{|c - c_1|}{\sqrt{a^2 + b^2}}$

Here $c_1 = 7$, $c_2 = -5$, $a = 3$, $b = 4$

so $d = \dfrac{|7 - (-5)|}{\sqrt{3^2 + 4^2}}$

$= \dfrac{12}{5}$

4. Application of Peter Chew Theorem for Geometry (Distance)

4.1 Distance between two points

Example 1 : What is the distance between two points A and B whose coordinates are $(1, 3)$ and $(2 + \sqrt{2}, \quad 5 + 2\sqrt{2})$, respectively?

Solution:

$$d = \sqrt{(x_2 - x_1)^2 + (y_2 - y_1)^2}$$

$$d = \sqrt{[(2 + \sqrt{2}) - 1]^2 + [(5 + 2\sqrt{2}) - 3]^2}$$

$$d = \sqrt{(1 + \sqrt{2})^2 + (2 + \sqrt{2})^2}$$

$$= \sqrt{3 + 2\sqrt{2} + 6 + 4\sqrt{2}}$$

$$= \sqrt{9 + 6\sqrt{2}}$$

$$= \sqrt{9 + 2\sqrt{18}}$$

$$d = \sqrt{9 + 2\sqrt{18}}$$

Current solution:

Let $\sqrt{9 + 2\sqrt{18}}$ be $\sqrt{x} + \sqrt{y}$

$$9 + 2\sqrt{18} = (\sqrt{x} + \sqrt{y})^2$$

$$= x + y + 2\sqrt{xy}$$

Comparing the two sides of the above equation,

We have $\quad x + y = 9$

$$y = 9 - x \dots i)$$

And $\quad\quad x\,y = 18 \quad \dots\dots ii)$

Substitute *i) in ii)*, $\quad x\,(9 - x) = 18$

$$9x - x^2 = 18$$

$$x^2 - 9x + 18 = 0$$

$$(x - 6)(x - 3) = 0$$

$$x = 6, 3$$

From *i*),

When x = 6, y = 9 − 6 = 3

When x = 3, y = 9 − 3 = 6

$$\sqrt{9 + 2\sqrt{18}} \;=\; \sqrt{6} + \sqrt{3}$$

$$\therefore \quad d = \sqrt{6} + \sqrt{3}$$

iii)   Peter Chew Theorem

Cause $x^2 - 9x + 18 = 0,$

then x = 6, 3

$$\therefore \;\sqrt{9 + 2\sqrt{18}} = \sqrt{6} + \sqrt{3}$$

$$\therefore \quad d = \sqrt{6} + \sqrt{3}$$

Example 1 : What is the distance between two points A and B whose coordinates are $(1, 3)$ and $(2 + \sqrt{2}, 5 + 2\sqrt{2})$, respectively?

Solution:

$d = \sqrt{(x_2 - x_1)^2 + (y_2 - y_1)^2}$

$d = \sqrt{[(2 + \sqrt{2}) - 1]^2 + [(5 + 2\sqrt{2}) - 3]^2}$

$d = \sqrt{(1 + \sqrt{2})^2 + (2 + \sqrt{2})^2}$

$= \sqrt{3 + 2\sqrt{2} + 6 + 4\sqrt{2}}$

$= \sqrt{9 + 6\sqrt{2}}$

$d = \sqrt{9 + 2\sqrt{18}}$

Current solution:

Let $\sqrt{9 + 2\sqrt{18}}$ be $\sqrt{x} + \sqrt{y}$

$9 + 2\sqrt{18} = (\sqrt{x} + \sqrt{y})^2$

$= x + y + 2\sqrt{xy}$

Comparing the two sides of the above equation,

We have $x + y = 9$

$y = 9 - x$ ..... i)

And $x y = 18$ ....ii)

Substitute i) in ii), $x(9-x) = 18$

$$9x - x^2 = 18$$

$$x^2 - 9x + 18 = 0$$

$$(x-6)(x-3) = 0$$

$$x = 6, 3$$

From i),

When $x = 6$, $y = 9 - 6 = 3$

When $x = 3$, $y = 9 - 3 = 6$

$$\sqrt{9 + 2\sqrt{18}} = \sqrt{6} + \sqrt{3}$$

∴   The distance is $\sqrt{6} + \sqrt{3}$

iii)   Peter Chew Theorem

Cause $x^2 - 9x + 18 = 0$,

then x = 6, 3

$\therefore \ \sqrt{9 + 2\sqrt{18}} = \sqrt{6} + \sqrt{3}$

$\therefore$ The distance is $\sqrt{6} + \sqrt{3}$

Example 2 : What is the distance between two points A and B whose coordinates are $(3, 7)$ and $(12 + 9\sqrt{2}, 25 + 9\sqrt{2})$, respectively?

Solution:

$$d = \sqrt{(x_2 - x_1)^2 + (y_2 - y_1)^2}$$

$$d = \sqrt{[(12 + 9\sqrt{2}) - 3]^2 + [(25 + 9\sqrt{2}) - 7]^2}$$

$$d = \sqrt{(9 + 9\sqrt{2})^2 + (18 + 9\sqrt{2})^2}$$

$$= \sqrt{243 + 162\sqrt{2} + 486 + 324\sqrt{2}}$$

$$= \sqrt{729 + 486\sqrt{2}}$$

$$d = \sqrt{729 + 2\sqrt{118\,098}}$$

Current solution:

Let $\sqrt{729 + 2\sqrt{118\ 098}}$ be $\sqrt{x} + \sqrt{y}$

$$729 + 2\sqrt{118\ 098} = (\sqrt{x} + \sqrt{y})^2$$

$$= x + y + 2\sqrt{xy}$$

Comparing the two sides of the above equation, we have, $x + y = 729$

$y = 729 - x$ ... *i)*

And $xy = 118\ 098$...*ii)*

Substitute *i)* **in** *ii),*

$$x(729 - x) = 118\ 098$$
$$x^2 - 729x + 118\ 098 = 0$$
$$(x - 486)(x - 243) = 0$$
$$x = 486, 243$$

From *i),* **When** $x = 486, y = 729 - 486 = 243$
When $x = 216, y = 729 - 243 = 486$

$$d = \sqrt{486} + \sqrt{243}$$
$$= 9\sqrt{6} + 9\sqrt{3}$$

The distance is $(9\sqrt{6} + 9\sqrt{3})$ Ω.

Peter Chew Theorem,

Cause $x^2 - 729x + 118\ 098 = 0$, then $x = 486, 243$

$$\therefore d = \sqrt{486} + \sqrt{243}$$
$$= 9\sqrt{6} + 9\sqrt{3}$$

The distance is $\left(9\sqrt{6} + 9\sqrt{3}\right)$.

Example 3

: What is the distance between two points A and B whose coordinates are (2, 5) and ($27 + 25\sqrt{3}$, $80 + 25\sqrt{3}$), respectively?

Solution:

$$d = \sqrt{(x_2 - x_1)^2 + (y_2 - y_1)^2}$$

$$d = \sqrt{[(27 + 25\sqrt{3}) - 2]^2 + [(80 + 25\sqrt{3}) - 5]^2}$$

$$d = \sqrt{(25 + 25\sqrt{3})^2 + (75 + 25\sqrt{3})^2}$$

$$= \sqrt{2\,500 + 1\,250\sqrt{3} + 7\,500 + 3\,750\sqrt{3}}$$

$$= \sqrt{10\,000 + 5\,000\sqrt{3}}$$

$$= \sqrt{10\,000 + 2\sqrt{18\,750\,000}}$$

$$d = \sqrt{10\,000 + 2\sqrt{18\,750\,000}}$$

Current solution:

Let $\sqrt{10\,000 + 2\sqrt{18\,750\,000}}$ be $\sqrt{x} + \sqrt{y}$

$$10\,000 + 2\sqrt{18\,750\,000} = (\sqrt{x} + \sqrt{y})^2$$

$$= x + y + 2\sqrt{xy}$$

Comparing the two sides of the above equation,

We have $\quad$ x + y = 10 000

$$y = 10\,000 - x \ \dots i)$$

And $\quad xy = 18\,750\,000 \ \dots ii)$

Substitute *i)* in *ii)*,

$$x\,(10\,000 - x) = 18\,750\,000$$

$$x^2 - 10\,000x + 18\,750\,000 = 0$$

$$(x - 7\,500)\,(x - 2\,500) = 0$$

$$x = 7\,500, \ 2\,500$$

From *i)*, When $x = 7\,500$, $y = 10\,000 - 7\,500 = 2\,500$

When $x = 2\,500$, $y = 10\,000 - 2\,500 = 7\,500$

$$d = \sqrt{7\,500} + \sqrt{2500}$$
$$= 50\sqrt{3} + 50$$

The distance is $(50 + 50\sqrt{3})$.

Peter Chew Theorem,

Cause $x^2 - 1000x + 18\,750\,000 = 0$, then $x = 2500, 7500$

$\therefore$ **d** $= \sqrt{2\,500} + \sqrt{7\,500}$
$= 50 + 50\sqrt{3}$

The distance is $(50 + 50\sqrt{3})$.

4.2 Distance between Point and Line

Example 1: Find the distance of the point (1, 0) from the line $(1 + \sqrt{2})x + (2 + \sqrt{2})y - 1 = 0$.

Solution:

Given line is $(1 + \sqrt{2})x + (2 + \sqrt{2})y - 1 = 0.$,

Given point is (1, 0).

The distance, $D = \dfrac{\left| (1+\sqrt{2})(1) + (2+\sqrt{2})(0) - 1 \right|}{\sqrt{(1+\sqrt{2})^2 + (2+\sqrt{2})^2}}$

$= \dfrac{\left| (1+\sqrt{2}) - 1 \right|}{\sqrt{3+2\sqrt{2}+6+4\sqrt{2}}}$

$= \dfrac{\sqrt{2}}{\sqrt{9+6\sqrt{2}}}$

$= \dfrac{\sqrt{2}}{\sqrt{9+2\sqrt{18}}}$

Current Method.

Let $\sqrt{9 + 2\sqrt{18}}$ be $\sqrt{x} + \sqrt{y}$

$$9 + 2\sqrt{18} = (\sqrt{x} + \sqrt{y})^2$$

$$= x + y + 2\sqrt{xy}$$

Comparing the two sides of the above equation,

We have $\quad x + y = 9$

$$y = 9 - x \ ..... \ i)$$

And $\qquad x\,y = 18 \ ....ii)$

Substitute $i)$ in $ii)$, $\quad x\,(9 - x) = 18$

$$9x - x^2 = 18$$

$$x^2 - 9x + 18 = 0$$

$$(x - 6)(x - 3) = 0$$

$$x = 6, \ 3$$

From $i)$,

When $x = 6$, $y = 9 - 6 = 3$

When $x = 3$, $y = 9 - 3 = 6$

$$\sqrt{9 + 2\sqrt{18}} = \sqrt{6} + \sqrt{3}$$

iii)   Peter Chew Theorem

Cause $x^2 - 9x + 18 = 0$,

then x = 6, 3

$\therefore \sqrt{9 + 2\sqrt{18}} = \sqrt{6} + \sqrt{3}$

$\therefore$ **The distance , D** $= \dfrac{\sqrt{2}}{\sqrt{9 + 2\sqrt{18}}}$

$$= \dfrac{\sqrt{2}}{\sqrt{6} + \sqrt{3}} \times \dfrac{\sqrt{6} - \sqrt{3}}{\sqrt{6} - \sqrt{3}}$$

$$= \dfrac{\sqrt{2} \times [\sqrt{6} - \sqrt{3}]}{(\sqrt{6})^2 - (\sqrt{3})^2}$$

$$= \dfrac{2[\sqrt{3} - \sqrt{6}]}{3}$$

Example 2: Find the distance of the point (2, 0) from the line

$(1 + \sqrt{2})x + (2 + \sqrt{2})y - 5 = 0.$

Solution:

Given line is $(4 + 4\sqrt{2})x + (8 + 4\sqrt{2})y - 5 = 0.,$

Given point is (2, 0).

The distance, $D = \dfrac{\left| (4+4\sqrt{2})(2) + (8 + 4\sqrt{2})(0) - 5 \right|}{\sqrt{(4+4\sqrt{2})^2 + (8+4\sqrt{2})^2}}$

$= \dfrac{\left| (8+8\sqrt{2}) - 5 \right|}{\sqrt{48+32\sqrt{2}+96+64\sqrt{2}}}$

$= \dfrac{3+8\sqrt{2}}{\sqrt{144+96\sqrt{2}}}$

$= \dfrac{3+8\sqrt{2}}{\sqrt{144+2\sqrt{4608}}}$

Current Method.

Let $\sqrt{144 + 2\sqrt{4608}}$ be $\sqrt{x} + \sqrt{y}$

$$144 + 2\sqrt{4608} = (\sqrt{x} + \sqrt{y})^2$$

$$144 + 2\sqrt{4608} = x + y + 2\sqrt{xy}$$

Comparing the two sides of the above equation,

we have, $x + y = 144$

$$y = 144 - x \dots i)$$

And $xy = 4608\dots ii)$

Substitute *i)* **in** *ii),* $\quad x(144 - x) = 4608$

$$x^2 - 144x + 4608 = 0$$

$$(x - 96)(x - 48) = 0$$

$$x = 96, 48$$

From *i),* **When** $x = 96, y = 144 - 96 = 48$

When $x = 48, y = 144 - 48 = 96$

$$\sqrt{144 + 2\sqrt{4608}} = \sqrt{96} + \sqrt{48}$$

$$= 4\sqrt{6} + 4\sqrt{3}$$

Peter Chew Theorems,

Cause $x^2 - 144x + 4608 = 0$, then $x = 96, 48$

$$\sqrt{144 + 2\sqrt{4608}} = \sqrt{96} + \sqrt{48}$$
$$= 4\sqrt{6} + 4\sqrt{3}$$

$\therefore$ The distance, $D = \dfrac{3+8\sqrt{2}}{4\sqrt{6} + 4\sqrt{3}}$.

$$= \frac{3+8\sqrt{2}}{4\sqrt{6} + 4\sqrt{3}} \times \frac{4\sqrt{6} - 4\sqrt{3}}{4\sqrt{6} - 4\sqrt{3}}$$

$$= \frac{[3+8\sqrt{2}] \times 4\,[\sqrt{6} - \sqrt{3}]}{(4\sqrt{6})^2 - (4\sqrt{3})^2}.$$

$$= \frac{4\,[3\sqrt{6} - 3\sqrt{3} + 8\sqrt{12} - 8\sqrt{6}\,]}{48}$$

$$= \frac{4\,[3\sqrt{6} - 3\sqrt{3} + 16\sqrt{3} - 8\sqrt{6}\,]}{48}$$

$$= \frac{13\sqrt{3} - 5\sqrt{6}}{12}$$

Example 3: Find the distance of the point (3, 0) from the line $(9 + 9\sqrt{2})$ x+ $(18+ 9\sqrt{2})$y -27 =0.

Solution:

Given line is $(9 + 9\sqrt{2})$ x $+ (18+ 9\sqrt{2})$y -27 = 0 ,Given point is (3, 0).

The distance , D $= \dfrac{\left| (9+9\sqrt{2})(3) + (18+9\sqrt{2})(0) - 27 \right|}{\sqrt{(9+9\sqrt{2})^2 + (18+9\sqrt{2})^2}}$

$= \dfrac{27\sqrt{2}}{\sqrt{729 + 486\sqrt{2}}}$

Current Method. **Let** $\sqrt{729 + 486\sqrt{2}}$ **be** $\sqrt{x} + \sqrt{y}$

$$729 + 486\sqrt{2} = (\sqrt{x} + \sqrt{y})^2$$

$$729 + 2\sqrt{118\,098} = x + y + 2\sqrt{xy}$$

Comparing the two sides of the above equation, we have, x +y = 729

y = 729- x ... i)

And $xy = 118\,098...ii)$

Substitute *i)* in *ii)*, $x(729 - x) = 118\ 098$

$$x^2 - 729x + 118\ 098 = 0$$

$$(x - 486)(x - 243) = 0$$

$$x = 486, 243$$

From *i)*, When $x = 486$, $y = 729 - 486 = 243$

When $x = 216$, $y = 729 - 243 = 486$

$$\sqrt{729 + 486\sqrt{2}} = \sqrt{486} + \sqrt{243}$$

$$= 9\sqrt{6} + 9\sqrt{3}$$

Peter Chew Theorems, **Cause $x^2 - 729x + 118\ 098 = 0$, then**

$x = 486, 243$

$$\sqrt{729 + 486\sqrt{2}} = \sqrt{486} + \sqrt{243}$$

$$= 9\sqrt{6} + 9\sqrt{3}$$

$\therefore$ The distance , $\mathbf{D} = \dfrac{27\sqrt{2}}{9\sqrt{6} + 9\sqrt{3}.}$

$$= \dfrac{27\sqrt{2}}{9\sqrt{6} + 9\sqrt{3}.} \times \dfrac{9\sqrt{6} - 9\sqrt{3}}{9\sqrt{6} - 9\sqrt{3}.}$$

$$= \dfrac{27\sqrt{2} \times [9\sqrt{6} - 9\sqrt{3}]}{(9\sqrt{6})^2 - (9\sqrt{3})^2.}$$

$$= \dfrac{243\sqrt{2} \times [\sqrt{6} - \sqrt{3}]}{243}$$

$$= 2\sqrt{3} - \sqrt{6}$$

4.3 Distance between Two Parallel Lines .

Example 1: Calculate the distance between the parallel lines
$(1 + \sqrt{3})x + (3 + \sqrt{3}) y + 3 = 0$ **and** $(1 + \sqrt{3})x + (3 + \sqrt{3}) y + 7 = 0.$

Solution:

The distance between two parallel lines is given by   d

$$= \frac{|c - c_1|}{\sqrt{a^2 + b^2}.}$$

The distance , D $= \dfrac{|7-3|}{\sqrt{(1+\sqrt{3})^2 + (3+\sqrt{3})^2.}}$

$$= \frac{4}{\sqrt{4 + 2\sqrt{3} + 12 + 6\sqrt{3}.}}$$

$$= \frac{4}{\sqrt{16 + 8\sqrt{3}}}$$

$$= \frac{4}{2\sqrt{4 + 2\sqrt{3}}}$$

$$= \frac{2}{\sqrt{4 + 2\sqrt{3}}}$$

Current Method.

Let $\sqrt{4 + 2\sqrt{3}}$ be $\sqrt{x} + \sqrt{y}$

$$\sqrt{4 + 2\sqrt{3}} = (\sqrt{x} + \sqrt{y})^2$$
$$4 + 2\sqrt{3} = x + y + 2\sqrt{xy}$$

Comparing the two sides of the above equation,

we have, $x + y = 4$

$$y = 4 - x \dots i)$$

And $xy = 3 \dots ii)$

Substitute *i)* in *ii)*, $\quad x(4 - x) = 3$

$$x^2 - 4x + 3 = 0$$
$$(x - 3)(x - 1) = 0$$
$$x = 3,\ 1$$

From *i)*,

When $x = 3$, $y = 4 - 3 = 1$

When $x = 1$, $y = 4 - 1 = 3$

$$\sqrt{4 + 2\sqrt{3}} = \sqrt{3} + \sqrt{1}$$
$$= \sqrt{3} + 1$$

Peter Chew Theorems,

Cause $x^2 - 4x + 3 = 0$, **then** $x = 3, 1$

$$\therefore \sqrt{4 + 2\sqrt{3}} = \sqrt{3} + \sqrt{1}$$

$$= \sqrt{3} + 1$$

$\therefore$ The distance , $D = \dfrac{2}{\sqrt{4 + 2\sqrt{3}}}$

$$= \dfrac{2}{\sqrt{3} + 1} \times \dfrac{\sqrt{3} - 1}{\sqrt{3} - 1}$$

$$= \dfrac{2 \times [\sqrt{3} - 1]}{(\sqrt{3})^2 - (1)^2.}$$

$$= \dfrac{2 \times [\sqrt{3} - 1]}{2.}$$

$$= \sqrt{3} - 1$$

Example 2: Calculate the distance between the parallel lines

$(1 + \sqrt{5})x + (5 + \sqrt{5})y + 5 = 0$ **and** $(1 + \sqrt{3})x + (3 + \sqrt{3})y + 8 = 0.$

Solution:

The distance between two parallel lines is given by   d

$$= \frac{|c - c_1|}{\sqrt{a^2 + b^2}}.$$

The distance , $D = \dfrac{|8 - 5|}{\sqrt{(1+\sqrt{5})^2 + (5+\sqrt{5})^2}}$.

$$= \frac{34}{\sqrt{6 + 2\sqrt{5} + 30 + 10\sqrt{5}}}.$$

$$= \frac{3}{\sqrt{36 + 12\sqrt{5}}}$$

$$= \frac{3}{\sqrt{36 + 2\sqrt{180}}}$$

Current Method.

Let $\sqrt{36 + 2\sqrt{180}}$ be $\sqrt{x} + \sqrt{y}$

$$\sqrt{36 + 2\sqrt{180}} = (\sqrt{x} + \sqrt{y})^2$$

$$36 + 2\sqrt{180} = x + y + 2\sqrt{xy}$$

Comparing the two sides of the above equation,

we have, $x + y = 36$

$$y = 36 - x \ ... \ i)$$

And $xy = 180 \ ...ii)$

Substitute *i)* **in** *ii)*, $\quad x(36 - x) = 180$

$$x^2 - 36x + 180 = 0$$

$$(x - 30)(x - 6) = 0$$

$$x = 30, \ 6$$

From *i)*,

When $x = 30, y = 36 - 30 = 6$

When $x = 6, \ y = 36 - 6 = 30$

$$\therefore \quad \sqrt{36 + 2\sqrt{180}} = \sqrt{30} + \sqrt{6}$$

Peter Chew Theorems,

Cause $x^2 - 36x + 180 = 0$, **then** $x = 30, 6$

$$\therefore \qquad \sqrt{36 + 2\sqrt{180}} = \sqrt{30} + \sqrt{6}$$

$\therefore$ The distance, $D = \dfrac{3}{\sqrt{36 + 2\sqrt{180}}}$

$$= \dfrac{3}{\sqrt{30} + \sqrt{6}} \times \dfrac{\sqrt{30} - \sqrt{6}}{\sqrt{30} - \sqrt{6}}$$

$$= \dfrac{3 \times [\sqrt{30} - \sqrt{6}]}{(\sqrt{30})^2 - (\sqrt{6})^2}$$

$$= \dfrac{3 \times [\sqrt{30} - \sqrt{6}]}{24}$$

$$= \dfrac{\sqrt{30} - \sqrt{6}}{8}$$

Example 3: Calculate the distance between the parallel lines $(25 + 25\sqrt{3})x + (75 + 25\sqrt{3})y + 5 = 0$ and $(25 + 25\sqrt{3})x + (75 + 25\sqrt{3})y + 25 = 0$.

Solution: The distance between two parallel lines is given by

$$d = \frac{|c - c_1|}{\sqrt{a^2 + b^2}.}$$

The distance , $D = \dfrac{|5-25|}{\sqrt{(25+25\sqrt{3})^2 +(75+25\sqrt{3})^2.}}$

$$= \frac{20}{\sqrt{2500 +1250\sqrt{3} +7\,500 +3750\sqrt{3}.}}$$

$$= \frac{20}{\sqrt{10\,000 +5000\sqrt{3}}}$$

Current Method. **Let** $\sqrt{10\,000 + 5\,000\sqrt{3}}$ **be** $\sqrt{x} + \sqrt{y}$

$$10\,000 + 5\,000\sqrt{3} = (\sqrt{x} + \sqrt{y})^2$$

$$10\,000 + 2\sqrt{18\,750\,000} = x + y + 2\sqrt{xy}$$

Comparing the two sides of the above equation,

we have, $x + y = 10\,000$

$$y = 10\,000 - x \dots i)$$

And $xy = 18\,750\,000 \dots ii)$

Substitute *i)* in *ii)*, $\quad x(10\,000 - x) = 18\,750\,000$

$$x^2 - 10\,000x + 18\,750\,000 = 0$$

$$(x - 7\,500)(x - 2\,500) = 0$$

$$x = 7\,500,\ 2\,500$$

From *i)*, When $x = 7\,500$, $y = 10\,000 - 7\,500 = 2\,500$

When $x = 2\,500$, $y = 10\,000 - 2\,500 = 7\,500$

$$\sqrt{10\,000 + 5\,000\sqrt{3}} = \sqrt{7\,500} + \sqrt{2500}$$

$$= 50\sqrt{3} + 50$$

Peter Chew Theorems, Cause $x^2 - 1000x + 18\,750\,000 = 0$,
then $x = 2500, 7500$

$$\therefore \sqrt{10\,000 + 5\,000\sqrt{3}} = \sqrt{2\,500} + \sqrt{7\,500}$$

$$= 50 + 50\sqrt{3}$$

$\therefore$ The distance, $D = \dfrac{20}{50 + 50\sqrt{3}}$

$$= \frac{\sqrt{3} - 1}{5}$$

5. Conclusion

The purpose of Peter Chew **Theorem** for Quadratic Surds is to let upcoming generation solve same problem of quadratic roots can solve simple and directly compare what`s now solution. Therefore, the application of Peter Chew theorem for Quadratic Surds in Geometry(Distance) can make the teaching and learning of Geometry(Distance) easier. The purpose of Peter Chew **Theorem** for Quadratic Surds is the same as Albert Einstein's famous quote **Everything should be made as simple as possible, but not simpler.**

In addition, Albert Einstein's also quote :

i)If you can't explain it simply you don't understand it well enough,

ii)We cannot solve our problems with the same thinking we used when we created them.

iii) When the solution is simple, God is answering

From the Albert Einstein's quote above, it can be seen that simplifying knowledge is very important.

6. Reference

[1]. Shefiu S. Zakariyah, PhD Surds Explained with Worked Examples. (26, 30) Feb.2014.
https://www.academia.edu/6086823/Surds_Explained_with_W orked_Examples

[2]. Peter Chew . Peter Chew Theorem and Application.

Chew, Peter, Peter Chew Theorem and Application (March 5, 2021). Available at SSRN: https://ssrn.com/abstract=3798498 or http://dx.doi.org/1 0.2139/ssrn.3798498.Europe PMC: PPR: PPR300039 .

[3] Agata Stefanowice, Joe Kyle, Michael Grove. Proofs and Mathematical Reasonung. University of Birmingham, September. 2014

[4]. Dr. Yibiao Pan. Mathematical Proofs and Their Importance. December 5, 2017

[5] **Distance between two points formula. BYJU`S**

https://byjus.com/maths/distance-between-two-points-formula/#:~:text=Distance%20between%20two%20points%20is,%E2%80%93%20y1)%C2%B2.

[6]   Hobart   Pao   et   all   .   BRILLIANT
https://brilliant.org/wiki/distance-between-point-and-line/

[7] Distance between 2 parallel lines example. **BYJU`S 2023.**
https://byjus.com/jee/distance-between-2-parallel-

Milton Keynes UK
Ingram Content Group UK Ltd.
UKHW020931231123
433129UK00016B/839